To Teresa, Leila, Joryn, Locke, and Briar Rose:

May your dreams be ever-sweet and marked by His love.

The Bedtime Book

Published by

Written by Devin Wright
Illustrated by Lizzie Masters

Contributions, Oversight & Overall Awesomeness by
Lindi Masters & Yeye Ikenna

The sun is asleep now, the stars sparkling bright.

My bedroom is dark, but my spirit is light.

The Mystery is calling, it's time for a rest.

The night holds the secrets, so bedtime's the best!

With my crown on my head and my sword at my right,

I close my eyes and I snuggle in tight…

The mysteries await me, what wonder they bring!

I go like a kid, yes, I go like a king!

The Father is calling me back where I'm from.

Up, up, and away, He beckons me, "Come!"

My belly will rest, my fingers and toes,

but my spirit will soar... watch out here it goes!

There are doors to new places for me to explore.

There are mountains, and rivers, and gemstones, and more...

Wait! There! Is that… sneak a peek if you can…

the Lion, the Ox, the Eagle, the Man!

The rainbows they dance at the sight of the King

The angels and saints join in and sing...

I dance to the music and join in the song

"Holy, Holy, Holy!" to Him I belong.

All glory, all honor, all praises I sing,

I lay down my crown to the King of all Kings!

His gaze catches mine and He gives me a grin,

"Well hello there," He says, as His love draws me in.

For the best of the secrets, I'll tell you a clue...

is that Father, He loves you! He's waiting for you!

Go meet Him at night where the mysteries dwell.

When morning is come, oh the things you can tell!

The sun is asleep now, the stars sparkling bright.

Let your little eyes rest, let your spirit take flight.

The sun is asleep now, the stars sparkling bright.

Let your little eyes rest, let your spirit take flight.

The mysteries are calling, and I tell you true...

He made the night time to spend time with you!

How To Use This Book
(A Caregiver's Guide)

What is the significance of the night time?

The Bedtime Book and My Bedtime Journal were created by MYSTKDZ in collaboration with kidZhub (Ignite Hubs International) to help lay a foundation for children (and care-givers!) to learn more about what is sometimes called the nightwatch. We call it the nightwatch because it is the special time where we allow our bodies to rest while we go into, watch, and learn the mysteries of the Kingdom of YHVH (Yahweh).

Psalm 119:148 My eyes stay open through the watches of the night, that I may meditate on your promises.

Psalm 63:6 On my bed I remember you; I think of you through the watches of the night.

Psalm 134:1 Behold, bless the LORD, all servants of the LORD, Who serve by night in the house of the LORD!

Psalm 119:62 At midnight I shall rise to give thanks to You Because of Your righteous ordinances.

How do I apply the principles of The Bedtime Book?

As you've probably noticed, children thrive off of having a routine. Having a predictable bedtime routine is one way that you can help your child have a good night's rest.

Similarly, we recommend incorporating the process of entering into the Kingdom Realms into your child's nightly routine. Not only can this help them in their bedtime routine, but also it will help create a well-worn path for them to engage the Kingdom during the daytime as well.

It is okay if there is some variation in how your child enters. For example: Some people see themselves entering through a curtain (the veil), while others see themselves enter through Yeshua's (Jesus') body and blood. Either way, we know that it is His body and blood that give us access so both are correct. Encourage them to enter the same way each time to help them in creating this pathway for engagement. They will find it will become easier and quicker with practice.

The Bedtime Book demonstrates how they can enter and some of the things they can see and engage with in the Kingdom. We encourage parents and caregivers to step in with them and engage together.

Why are dreams important?

We know that one of the ways that God speaks to us and teaches us is through dreams or visions of the night.

Matthew 2:13 Now when they had gone, behold, an angel of the Lord appeared to Joseph in a dream and said, "Get up! Take the Child and His mother and flee to Egypt, and remain there until I tell you; for Herod is going to search for the Child to destroy Him."

Acts 16:9 A vision appeared to Paul in the night: a man of Macedonia was standing and appealing to him, and saying, "Come over to Macedonia and help us.

Acts 2:17 In the last days, God says, I will pour out my Spirit on all people. Your sons and daughters will prophesy, your young men will see visions, your old men will dream dreams.

We have included My Dream Journal as part of the bedtime set to encourage your child to pay attention to what they are engaging and dreaming about. You can encourage your child as well by asking them if they had any dreams, or what they feel like YHVH was showing them in the night. Enjoy quality time with your little ones by drawing and learning alongside them.

Questions for learning...

Here are some other questions you can ask your children concerning The Bedtime Book:

1. Why do you think she has a sword and a crown? Do you have one?
2. How can her body and spirit be in different places at the same time?
3. Have you ever had dreams full of mystery and adventure?
4. Is there a time that you felt like God was trying to talk to you in your dreams?
5. Why is she laying down her crown for God
6. Why does Father want to share His Kingdom with us?

Z z z Sweet Dreams!

"The Bedtime Book" Copyright © 2019

Written by Devin Wright

Illustrated by Lizzie Masters

A special thank you to Lindi Masters, Yeye Ikenna, and Lizzie Masters

Thank you to Ignite Hubs International for your ongoing support and assistance.

Special Recognition to Ian Clayton and Lindi Masters.

Thank you for your faithfulness in sharing the mystery.

Published by Seraph Creative in 2018
ISBN 978-0-6399841-3-1

All rights reserved. © No part of this publication may be reproduced or used in any manner without the written permission of the copyright holder.

www.ingramcontent.com/pod-product-compliance
Lightning Source LLC
Chambersburg PA
CBHW041155290426
44108CB00002B/77